My Toaster's Grandfather

A Simple Look at Lean Operations from a
Toaster's Point of View – One Slice at a Time

By

Ronald and Lucinda Buckley

Published by
Shady Brook Press
Norwalk, CT

Other Books by the Author

Winning in a Highly Competitive
Manufacturing Environment,
Ronald L Buckley

No Eraser Needed
Mistake Proofing Your Business
Ronald L and Candace Lynn Buckley

Winning Manufacturing Solutions
Optimizing Performance with Lean Strategies
Ronald and Lucinda Buckley

My Toaster's Grandfather

A Simple Look at Lean Operations from a
Toaster's Point of View – One Slice at a Time

Copyright © 2012

By

Ronald L Buckley

ISBN-13: 978-1477522202
ISBN-10: 1477522204

Published by
Shady Brook Press
14 Shady Brook Lane
Norwalk, Ct 06854

Dedication

I dedicate this effort to the marvelous men and women that I have had the great privilege of working with over the last 30 plus years. I also acknowledge their contribution to this work. I profoundly hope that this book conveys the tremendous respect and gratitude I have for these people and their efforts.

Acknowledgment

A special thanks to the late Tom Reynolds, a dynamic dedicated leader at The Raytheon Company, a teacher who motivated his employees to reach beyond their comfort zones and try new ideas. Tom encouraged the pursuit of Lean operating ideas long before they became popular or even acceptable.

A special thanks to John Wiig for his help and support in this effort.

Cover design by John H Wiig.

Content

Prologue   13

Chapter 1
Nice to Meet You!   17

Chapter 2
Different Beginnings   23

Chapter 3
Sally's Mistake Proofing Program   35

Chapter 4
Sally's Lean Factory   59

Chapter 5
Sally's Teams   72

Epilogue:
A Final Word   91

Glossary of Terms   93

Appendix A   101
Appendix B   113
Appendix C   123
Appendix D   127

Prologue

This short story is told by a toaster who was created in the same factory as his Grandfather. Contrasts are made between how the Grandfather and Grandson were created and adopted into their current home. For a time they sit side-by-side on the same counter and share stories of how they were built – Grandfather's coils are twice as thick as his Grandson's and he was built to last, as he was built at a time when toasters were a relatively expensive item. However, these are different times and competition has made it necessary to cut costs. In fact, our toaster never got to know his parents because they were early failures – the result of cutting corners that degraded product quality and drove the toaster factory to the brink of bankruptcy.

Our toasters live with Sally who along with her husband Bill, has taken responsibility for fixing her Father's factory. Sally and Bill spend a lot of time in the kitchen talking about how they are using Lean methodologies and employee empowerment to convert the company to a highly profitable lean moneymaking business. This book makes these concepts, which tend to be **unnecessarily** complicated, easier to understand by all. The book's intended audience is virtually anybody involved in the process of delivering any product or service.

Chapter 1

Chapter 1
Nice to Meet You!

I want to tell you about my ancestors and how I came into being. My Grandfather was a grand old toaster – capable of doing four slices in less than two minutes. His heating coils were twice as thick as mine and he weighed three times what I do.

He was manufactured in the same factory I was, when the toaster factory occupied 400,000 square feet of space in St. Louis, Missouri. Almost all of his parts were made in the same factory. Mine were made in 14 different factories. He had twice as many parts as I do. It took 16 weeks from the time his first part, the mainframe, was made until he finally was made whole and ready to take his rightful place in a Finished Goods Stockroom along with all the other proud toasters waiting several weeks for their turn to be shipped off to a lonely distribution center.

He went on to a store to be eventually taken home by a caring family, where he would serve their every toasting need for years to come. I was created in less than one hour in the same factory; however, only 85,000 square feet of the factory was dedicated to manufacturing. I was then shipped directly to my new home the same day I was created.

It just so happens that my Grandfather's home is the same home that I was adopted into. At first I had the great honor to sit right next to my Grandfather. It was so wonderful just being near him – feeling the warmth from him as his strong coils warmed that counter top.

He was with me long enough to teach me everything I needed to know about toasting to perfection. Just how little Bobby liked his muffins and how Bobby's little sister, Susie, liked her bagels. Their Mother and Father always liked their rye toasted lightly. What fun we had in those early days with our adopted family. Grandpa is still here, but he's been moved to the guesthouse. Now we only get to see each other at large family events when they need both of us to serve all the guests. Before he left for his post in the guesthouse, he told me all about how he was made. He had a much different beginning than I.

I did not know my Mother or my Father. My Grandfather says they were both early quality failures. I was once worried I would suffer the same fate; however, my Grandfather said that I had nothing to worry about because I was designed and built with Six Sigma quality techniques.

Six Sigma techniques sounded very complex to me when my Grandfather first mentioned them. I later found out that many of these techniques are quite simple to understand and use.

This means that some of the tools that were used to create me came out of a very different kind of tool box than the tools that were used to create my Grandfather. They call it the Six Sigma Tool Box, which is more like a locker of ideas and methodologies like Mistake Proofing and a set of statistical tools that help to eliminate variation in the manufacturing process. These tools are used in conjunction with the mechanical assembly tools – like power screwdrivers, socket wrenches and welding machines – that were used to create my Grandfather.

I am very lucky that I have a good memory and can remember all the steps taken to make me what I am today. My Grandfather is equally blessed with an excellent memory. He not only taught me how to toast to perfection, but he also told me all about how he was created – each and every step. We were able to take advantage of the time we spent together in that grand kitchen trading stories about our creation.

I am so lucky that he's still around, since most toasters from his generation are no longer around. My generation faired much better – most of us are still creating masterpieces from whatever we are given to toast.

Chapter 2

Chapter 2

Different Beginnings

This is what I remember about our creation – let's begin. The order to create my Grandfather, called a "work order," was generated from a forecast that the Sales Department in New York gave the Production Planning group in the factory in St. Louis, Missouri. The order to make 4,000 toasters just like my Grandfather went to the "Parts Stockroom," also known as the "Kitting Area," where all the parts were pulled from many bins and placed on skids that would later be sent to the main assembly area as a "kit." Some of the parts, like his mainframe, had been made weeks before on other "work orders" that called for large quantities called "economic order quantities." These parts just sat around in the parts stockroom until they were needed in a kit to fill a forecasted requirement on a "work order." I still don't understand why they called the order quantities economic – they were anything but.

Forecast accuracy was one reason my Grandfather had to wait so long first in the Finished Goods Stockroom, then the Distribution Center and finally the store shelf before being adopted into a home. Grandpa says a forecast is something that may or may not happen in the future … and usually never does. He and his friends learned this from first-hand experience waiting around in all those lonely places before finding a home.

In contrast to my Grandfather's "work order," I was ordered by my adopted family directly over the internet before my first part was made. No Forecast, No work order, No Kitting, No Waiting in the Finished Goods Area, No waiting in the Warehouse, No waiting in the Distribution Center and No waiting on the Store Shelf. Grandpa and I estimated this sitting around added up to about 14 weeks. Add this to his 16 week assembly time and you have a total creation time of thirty weeks before my Grandfather was placed in his home.

My Grandfather's assembly time took 16 weeks because of parts shortages. His assembly had begun only to discover that there was a problem with two main parts: the handles and the coils. His handles arrived two weeks late from the molding area because of set-up problems and his coils were rejected by an Incoming Parts Inspector, being one of the few parts that came from an outside vendor. His coils had to wait one week for paperwork before they could begin their journey back to their manufacturer in Texas. Once his coils were received by their manufacturer in Texas, the process to repair the minor defect in the tumbler only took minutes, but it took another two weeks to process the repair order and work the repair into the Texas vendor's factory schedule. Once the repair work was complete, it took three days to ship his coils back to my Grandfather's factory where they again had to sit and wait their turn for incoming inspection. After inspection, the coils had to be stocked in the stockroom, then pulled from their storage bin to fill the kit shortage on the production floor.

Once all his parts were present they had to be rescheduled for final assembly. When all his parts were present and ready to go, it only took two hours for his creation. But he then had to wait, *again*, at the Final Assembly Inspection station for another day to be inspected before he could be packaged for the Finished Goods storage area.

Wow, in fact all of his parts had to wait at many points in their creation for inspectors to inspect them. Between the waiting for inspection, the actual inspection time, the assembly time, the waiting for parts shortages to be filled and the actual assembly time it took 16 weeks for his creation.

Many of the parts in the same batches that my Grandfather's parts were selected from were rejected. They had to be scrapped or reworked at great expense. The factory my Grandfather was created in had 30 inspectors. This didn't include any inspectors in the factories that supplied his purchased parts.

The factory I was created in had zero inspectors on its production lines. All of my parts were designed and manufactured with

Six Sigma methodologies. The processes that created my parts were capable of making a good part on a repeatable basis. The manufacturing process itself served as the inspection. The processes were Mistake Proofed – this means that either each and every part that went into my creation was made so that any defect was immediately detectable and fixed or the process was designed so that it was not possible to make a mistake (defective part).

I learned this from Sally. She was a wonderful person in charge of the factory's Mistake Proofing and Lean Manufacturing programs – more about Sally later.

My mainframe was made in a work cell right in back of the final assembly cell that I was created in. When my mainframe was needed, a signal was sent to the work cell next door. No separate "work order" was needed and when the container containing my mainframe was removed from the work cell next door, it left only one container containing 50 mainframes. This meant that it was time for 50 more mainframes just like mine to be made. When the container my mainframe was in was removed, it left an empty space that was easy for all the workers in the work cell next door to see.

Sally also implemented this system. She is such a smart person.

Some of my parts came from other factories. In fact, my coils came from the same factory that my Grandfather's coils came from. However, Sally insisted that they get onboard with her quality programs, so guess what – no more defects. It wasn't easy convincing the coil vendor, but eventually they came around after being faced with losing Sally's business. Sally and some of her helpers had to spend time helping the coil vendor set up their own programs. After the program was up and running, they were so grateful that they reduced the price of the coils and still doubled their profits. All their other customers were very happy too!

As I promised earlier, I will now tell you about Sally. I first met Sally the day I was created. Sally is the Lean Leader in the factory I was created in and her husband, Bill, manages the factory. It just so happens that they are the family that adopted me through the internet. Of course, Sally is not aware that

I am that toaster that was created in her factory on that day, because toasters are not permitted to talk to people. You see, since my Grandfather and I both live with Sally and Bill, we are privileged to be able to learn much about how they create toasters. They talk about manufacturing all the time. It is their favorite subject after little Bobby and little Susie (their two children).

Sally and Bill are so proud of their factory. Their profits have doubled in the last few years and the cost to create me is less than half the cost it was to create my Grandfather.

Most important is how happy their employees are. They love the Self-Directed Team approach. Each and every employee is happily involved in the factory's improvement process and thus they have a lot of control over their future. Most of the employees have now been trained to do several different tasks that can vary widely like assembly, testing or welding. They love having many different skill sets. But the story was not always this good.

When Sally inherited the toaster company from her father, it was on the verge of going out of business. Each year things seemed to get progressively worse. The factory was losing $5,000,000 a year on $100,000,000 in annual sales. First pass yield (the number of toasters, including their sub-assemblies, which passed inspection at every stage of their creation the first time) was at 62%. Inventory was at $24,000,000. There were 30 shop floor inspectors on the manufacturing floor. Cycle time to make a toaster – including components and sub-assemblies – was 16 weeks. There were many parts shortages that caused delays all the time and the factory was driven by "work orders."

Sally was given a directive by her bankers – Fix the factory or close it. The factory had been her father's pride and joy. Sally grew up knowing all the families that worked in her father's factory; they were like her family, too. Closing the factory was never an option for Sally. She had to find a way to turn the factory around.

Sally's father had made high-end toasters for years. It was easy to pass on increasing costs to customers that were willing to pay. There was little to no competition; a toaster was recognized as a relatively high cost appliance in the American household and a toaster made in the USA was the only option. One would not consider buying a toaster made outside the USA.

Then things began to change little by little. Cheaper components, out sourcing and foreign competition drove the average cost to make a toaster down to five dollars. It became tougher and tougher to compete. The result was a factory producing poor quality products from cheaper components while losing more and more money each year.

Sally met Bill at college, where they were both studying Manufacturing Engineering. After they were married. Bill continued his education and received his MBA. Sally continued to focus on Manufacturing Engineering, learning things like Lean Manufacturing and Six Sigma. Sally's family hired Bill to manage the toaster business and Sally took over as the Lean Leader in the factory. She was always reading books like: *Zero Quality Control: Source Inspection and the Poka-yoke System*, *Winning in a Highly Competitive Manufacturing Environment* and *Mistake Proofing Your Business*. She became a certified Six Sigma black belt. Most importantly she learned about Self-Directed Teams from one of her professors who helped her get started on the path to fixing the toaster factory.

Sally's efforts have been very successful. It took the whole Team working together to pull it off, but the rewards have been great for everyone. First pass yields improved from 62% to well over 99% and this is without any Shop Floor Inspectors, who were given other jobs in the factory. Total inventory was under $7,000,000. Cycle time to make a toaster, including components and sub-assemblies, was down to less than one day. A part shortage was a very unusual thing and when a shortage did occur, it was resolved quickly. The "work orders" have been replaced by a "Demand Pull Manufacturing" system. And best of all a loss of $5,000,000 per year has been replaced by profits of $18,000,000 a year; while at the same time, sales have increased from $100,000,000 to $140,000,000.

Chapter 3

Chapter 3

Sally's Mistake Proofing Program

Sally's Mistake Proofing Program involved each and every employee in both the factory and the office. What fun the employees were having mistake proofing the business! Everybody's ideas were important and everyone was excited to be making contributions. By the time I was created the program had been well established. The idea that mistakes were caused more by flaws in processes, than by the people performing the processes, was very popular with all the workers.

Sally says that prior to her Mistake Proofing Program, the working environment was not very friendly. By the time I came along, the folks that created me with care seemed very happy working together.

Before Sally got involved the 30 Shop Floor Inspectors would inspect the work of their assembly associates in batches of hundreds of parts, dozens of assemblies and lots of finished toasters. Very often, they would find defects and sometimes entire lots of items had to be reworked or scrapped in large batches. None of the assembly associates liked being told the work they had just done was bad – this created animosity between the inspectors and the assemblers, and between the more skilled workers and the less skilled workers. After all they were just doing the best they could with the tools, materials and processes they were dealt. Sure some with superior skills did better than others, but not everyone was blessed with superior skills.

Sally says that a well-designed process should be able to be performed correctly regardless of skill level. By the time I was created there were no inspectors and the processes were designed to either check each item that was made immediately as the process was completed or the process was designed so that a defect was impossible. This coupled with the belief that none of their employees got up in the morning and said "I am going to work today to make all the mistakes I can," serves as the premise for the Mistake Proofing Program. The nice part was that the same employees that did the work were the ones that changed the process from the old system to the new system. They all had great fun working together to make the factory a fun place to work.

The training was ongoing. New employees were trained before they were certified to work in each work cell. This insured that only skilled hands were involved in my creation – a very pleasant experience indeed. Other employees were given refresher courses regularly and Sally kept track of the program's progress. Many employees were rewarded with recognition and some even received small gifts for their ideas. Knowing that their ideas were appreciated encouraged them to participate even more. Imagine the power of all the minds in the factory trying to improve what they did every day. Sally calls this "employee empowerment" – employees seemed to love having some control over the work they do.

Of course, Sally gets credit for teaching the skills needed to mistake proof the factory's processes. First, each employee was taught that even 100% inspection would not catch all the defects. She did this by asking each trainee to inspect all the words in a paragraph and count a certain letter that appeared often in the paragraph. Almost no one got the correct number of letters. This was just one way to demonstrate why relying on inspectors to check the quality of another employee's work is not very effective.

After Sally's Mistake Proofing Program was in place, the improvement in quality was so dramatic that eventually all the inspectors were given other jobs in the factory. The quality improvements even drove more sales, and helped support the new longer-term warranty offered to customers.

Sally taught that everyone makes mistakes. She says that common sense solutions can Mistake Proof all the factory's processes so that mistakes will be prevented. Everyone working in the factory is capable of applying common sense solutions to each and every process to eliminate mistakes. Unless a process can be performed by any properly trained employee – not just those with exceptional talent – it is not a capable process and must be mistake proofed and made capable of performing without variation on a repeatable basis.

Sally used examples of Mistake Proofing that all employees frequently encounter, are familiar with and, therefore, could easily relate to like circuit breakers in their homes, grocery store scanners that eliminate the possibility of a checkout person making an entry error and childproof locks in their homes or cars. All of these are the highest level of Mistake Proofing in that they completely prevent errors if used correctly. If a circuit breaker is off, no current can flow thereby preventing a shock if exposed to a short. Like the day I was toasting little Bobby's muffins and he put his toy truck into my coils – the circuit breaker kicked off and stopped the flow of electricity. We were both shaken up but unhurt. When the grocery store scanner scans the barcode, the price connected to the barcode is registered and the inventory is relieved at the same time – no possibility for human error. If the child-proof lock is set correctly on the rear doors of the car, the child cannot open the door by mistake.

There are other mistake-proofing methods that help prevent errors but do not completely eliminate the possibility of an error such as buzzers, warning lights and indicator gauges. When a mistake-proofing method that completely eliminates the possibility of making a mistake is not readily available, Sally encouraged everyone to use these and other warning devices that tell us an error has just occurred or is about to occur to improve a process and then keep working on improving the process until a method that does completely eliminate the possibility of making an error is developed. Sometimes we are forced to use a less desirable method because the best error preventing method costs too much to implement. Again, Sally says go ahead and use the less desirable method, but keep looking for a low-cost method that completely eliminates the possibility of making an error. Most of the mistake-proofing methods are quick and easy to implement at low cost, especially when compared to making defects that cause expensive scrap and rework.

Sally used many examples to teach the factory's employees the tools and methods of mistake proofing. Easy to use tools and methods like: using the shape of the design so parts fit only one way, such as notched parts; weighing scales to check for presence, volume or size; counters to check for quantity and presence; pass through holes checking for size; and templates to insure access to the correct items. Some other tools and methods Sally's Teams utilized required some assistance to implement but were very effective in preventing errors in the toaster factory. They included: motion detectors checking for movement and presence; bar-coding to prevent entry errors; contact devices checking for presence; photo cells checking for presence, size, quantity or quality; using components as conductors that power equipment (if the component is not present or is defective the equipment stops for lack of power); comparative databases that check for equivalent or non-equivalent data. Still other tools and methods may not *completely* eliminate errors but will greatly decrease the possibility of an error occurring such as: using colors as a form of identification and distinction; method sheets with pictures as well as assembly models for assemblers; statistical control charts that monitor the process to insure that the process remains in control.

Sally says "one of the nicest parts of mistake proofing is that it is fun work." No engineering degree is required, only common sense. Everyone can get into the act. The next blockbuster idea can come from anyone. Employees from all levels of the organization and all walks of life get to work together resolving problems. This lowers costs and improves quality; what a great way to apply an employee's talents and energy and they love it. She calls this the *Fun Factor*.

Problem-Solving Tools and Techniques

Problem-solving tools and techniques are an important part of any mistake-proofing program. Sally says to keep them simple so that all employees can understand and use them. She started by teaching employees how to use the following:

Cause and Effects Diagram

The cause and effect diagram (sometimes called the fishbone diagram) is very effective yet easy to understand. An example is on the next page:

Cause and Effect Diagram (Fishbone)

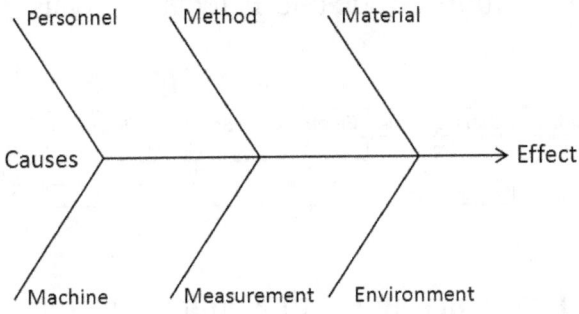

Each possible cause is analyzed to determine its contribution to the effect. Sally says this technique is easy to use and easy to understand. When the problem (the effect) is placed at the head and the possible causes of the problem are listed on the legs, each cause can be analyzed for its contribution to the problem. This can lead to the discovery of solutions.

Failure Mode and Effects Analysis

This is one of Sally's favorites. This tool is also simple to use and understand. It only takes a little practice to become fond of the Failure Mode and Effects Analysis tool. See the example below:

FMEA

Failure Mode and Effects Analysis

Problem	Consequence	Frequency	Severity	Detection	Score
Shard	Short	4	10	5	**200**
Rock	Short	2	10	5	100
Lint	Unknown	1	2	5	10

Problem – in the first column list the problem. On the first line in this example the problem is the presence of a sharp shard. **Consequence** – the consequences of the presence of a sharp shard is an electrical short. **Frequency** – on a scale of 1 to 10, 1 being the lowest, the frequency of this occurring is ranked as a 4. In other words there is a 4 in 10 chance of a sharp shard being present and that shard, causing an electrical short`. **Severity** – on a scale of 1 to

10, 1 being the lowest, the severity of a shard causing an electrical short is ranked as a 10. In this case a short renders the item useless; hence, the most severe condition gets a rank of 10. **Detection** – on a scale of 1 to 10, 1 being the lowest, the difficulty of detecting a shard that would cause a short is ranked as a 5. There is a 50% chance that the presence of a shard that would create a short would not be detected before it created a short; therefore, it received a rank of 5 – 5 being 50% of 10. **Score** – to determine the score simply multiply the Frequency times the Severity times the Detection and enter the result in the score column. In this case 4 x 10 x 5 = 200. Repeat this for the other problems identified, list the results in descending order by score. Address the problems that get the highest score first. You may choose not to address problems that receive a very low score.

There are certain characteristics of a problem that would cause it to receive a low score. A very low rank for frequency, severity or detection, like a score of 1, would result in a fairly low overall score. For instance: a rank of 4 for frequency, 10 for severity and a 1 for detection would result in a total score of only 40. 4 x 10 x 1 = 40. In this example the problem is highly detectable so the consequences can be mitigated by detection, hence a low score of 40. You will want to fix the problem in time, but it will probably not be your most pressing problem needing immediate attention.

On the other hand, if detection had received a rank of 10 – meaning that the presence of a shard causing a short is not detectable the total score would have been 400 (4 x 10 x 10). The much higher score of 400 requires immediate action. A high detection rank of 10 gives us a hint that part of a mitigating solution may be to come up with a method of detecting the problem before it can cause an electrical short.

Sally says that with a little practice this is an excellent tool to add to anyone's problem-solving tool box – easily explained and easily understood. Someone who has had little exposure to these types of tools may find using this technique a bit formidable at first. However, after the tool is used just a few times, almost anyone will become comfortable with failure mode and effects analysis.

Pareto Analysis

Pareto analysis is based on the rule that in a great many cases 80% of the consequences are the result of 20% of the causes. Do not take the rule literally it could just as easily be that 85% of the consequences are the result of 15% of the causes. Sally says, "… what is important here is to recognize that a few items can cause the majority of the consequences." If you accept this rule, how does this help you find solutions to problems? Easily, by categorizing and ranking a group of causes you are analyzing the possible causes or at the very least determining which causes probably have the most effect on the problem.

Simple and easy to understand, Pareto is another nice tool for the problem-solving toolbox.

Brainstorming

Sally calls this one of the most powerful tools. Brainstorming is an excellent method of coming up with solutions to problems. To get her point across, Sally says, "I have never met an individual who is smarter than 10 dumb people in a room and I know a lot of very smart people." You may think this statement is a bit dramatic; however, she would ask you to think about it before you jump to that conclusion. She says that there is something kind of magical that happens when you get a group of people together to brainstorm.

In a brainstorming session someone throws out an idea. That idea spurs someone else in the group to get an idea that he or she never would have come up with had he or she not heard the idea previously thrown out. Multiply this times 10 people and the sum is truly greater than the whole. *This is the power of brainstorming.*

In a brainstorming session a group of folks sit around a table and brainstorm for ideas. As the ideas are brought up, they are recorded. Some groups use flip charts, others groups use file cards or record the ideas on a computer that is projected on a screen. Sally likes to use flip charts for recording the ideas so that they can be taped to the walls for all participants to reference as the session progresses.

Sally says that it is important that all ideas be respected, especially unpopular ideas – often the minority ideas bring with them the most effective solutions. After all, if the solutions were so obvious, why would Sally need to hold a brainstorming session? The brainstorming should continue until either no more ideas are forthcoming or the ideas that are forthcoming are really dumb ones. At this point the brainstorming portion of the work is called complete by the brainstorming leader and hopefully the best solution to the problem is apparent.

In the event that several different solutions emerge for the same problem, Sally likes to categorize them in a four blocker like the one below on the next page.

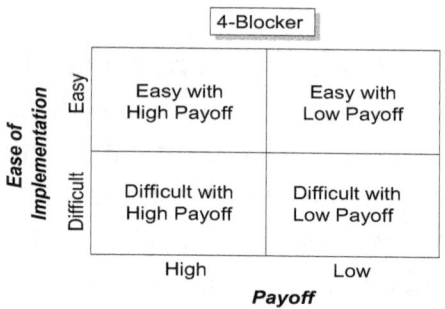

Ideas that are easy to execute with a high payoff go in the upper left quadrant.

Ideas that are easy to implement but have a low payoff go in the upper right quadrant.

Ideas that are difficult to implement with a high payoff go in the lower left quadrant.

Ideas that are difficult to execute with a low payoff go in the bottom right quadrant.

Next, pick the idea or combination of ideas that will give you the highest-level solution to your mistake-proofing problem and will be the least difficult to implement.

Six Sigma

Both Statistical Process Control (SPC) and mistake-proofing (Poka-yoke) are Six Sigma tools, as is Failure Mode Effects Analysis (FMEA) and the other problem-solving techniques. Sally and her Team use all of these tools. Of course, each of these tools can be used separately and do not have to be part of a Six Sigma program.

Many smaller organizations will shy away from a full-blown Six Sigma program, which can be expensive and difficult to implement. Six Sigma requires a much more complex infrastructure for training and a much larger resource commitment for support than does a mistake-proofing program. Sally says "sure it would be nice if the resources were available for a full-blown Six Sigma program; however, much progress can be made using the simpler tools such as mistake-proofing." So in our smaller organization, Sally started with a Mistake Proofing Program. After she collected from the payoff of those efforts she moved on to Six Sigma.

One point Sally likes to make is "While a Six Sigma quality level would be 3.4 failures per million opportunities, we should not stop until there are zero defects. Of course, we should always consider an improvement's practicality while taking cost into consideration."

When Sally first took over as the Factory Lean Leader, she was confronted with a serious problem – complete product failures leading to a total product recall and total shut down of the manufacturing facility.

On her first day she convened a meeting bringing together about 20 of this company's best and brightest (virtually all were degreed Engineers and some had advanced degrees). She was told that they were sure they knew what the problem was. The culprit was a sharp metal shard on the mainframe that was piercing the coil to short out and cause the toaster to fail completely. At that point she said to herself "Self I will have this one licked in less than five days." Well, things didn't quite go the way she thought they would at first. When she asked to see the data, she was told that they had no data, but they knew the problem was metal shards on the mainframe piercing the coils. She then asked the Team to collect the data. She was told that this would take a few days. They called the meeting to an end and agreed to reconvene a few days later when the field returns had been inspected and the data had been collected.

When the Team reconvened days later, she was told that they did not have all the data yet; however, now they were sure that sharp metal shards were less than 50% of the problem. She knew then that her dream of a speedy solution was lost. In the end sharp metal shards did *not* cause any of the failures. The problem was the torque pressure used in assembling components to the mainframe.

The approach that Sally used to bring her father's company back from the brink was simply to apply Six Sigma methodology in the broadest sense. She insisted that the Team follow the DMAIC method – Define, Measure, Analyze, Improve and Control.

Define the problem – in the shard case, defining the problem correctly would have gone a long way toward solving the problem, leading to a mistake-proofed solution.

Measuring – collecting and measuring the data.

Analyze – analyze the data collected.

Improve – improve the process/product.

Control – put controls in place to assure that the solution continues to be effective.

The result was to bring some structure to the company's problem-solving approach allowing the real causes of problems to be ferreted out and fixed rather than just treating the symptoms.

The problem was identified, fixed and mistake-proofed. Sally's Company resumed manufacturing and successfully replaced all customer products that had failed.

These are only a *few* of the many problem-solving tools and techniques Sally has in her tool box that can be used in the mistake-proofing process. They were selected because they are particularly helpful, easy to explain and easy to understand. Sally encourages the Teams to explore the use of other problem-solving tools and techniques. Meanwhile these served to get Sally's program under way.

On the last day of each training session, Sally's Teams – armed with their new skills, went right to work finding processes to mistake-proof in her factory. Within hours the Team had many ideas and within a few days many of the ideas were implemented.

Chapter 4

Chapter 4

Sally's Lean Factory

Responsibility

Sally believes that all employees have to be engaged in improving the business every working day. She says "It's every employee's responsibility to generate profits for their investors, provide a healthy happy working environment for all the company's workers and perpetuate the business." Perpetuating the business means executing on those things that insure the company's future like continuous improvement to insure that customers receive a quality product at a competitive price when they want it, as well as, being a good corporate citizen while using resources efficiently and eliminating waste.

Lean Continuous Improvement

To bring about the change, which would turn her company around, Sally engaged all employees in a lean continuous improvement program through Cross-Functional Self-Directed Teams. Again, education and training was a key to the success of this effort.

From Push to Pull
Eliminate "Work Orders"

The boldest step was moving from a "work order" push manufacturing system to a demand-driven pull manufacturing system. "Work orders" were eliminated one at a time and replaced with a signaling system that signaled it was time to make more components, sub-assemblies or assemble finished toasters.

This is how it works: A small number of toasters were kept in the finished goods area – only enough to cover incoming customer orders while replacements were being assembled. The toasters were stored in bins of 20. When a bin was emptied to fill customer orders, the empty bin was sent to the assembly cell that manufactured that type of toaster. The arrival of the empty bin served as the signal to make more toasters. As sub-assemblies and components were removed from their shelves, the bins they were in were sent to the area where they were manufactured. This then served as a signal to make more components and/or sub-assemblies.

Some signals were sent to outside vendors electronically, using the internet to communicate with the suppliers. Some signals were delivered by Kanban cards directly to vendors who had been given space to setup in-house stockrooms right in the toaster factory. The cards were kept with the parts and were delivered to the vendors when a certain quantity of parts was reached – the order point.

The order point was determined by the quantity of parts needed to cover production requirements while waiting for the vendor to deliver the Kanban quantity. The Kanban quantity was the agreed upon quantity that would be supplied by the vendor each time he/she received a signal for that part.

The order point and the Kanban quantity can differ greatly. Take my coils for example – the cell I was created in made 80 toasters, just like me, in an hour. It took the in-house store a maximum of just four hours to deliver more coils. The order point was set at 320 coils – 80 coils an hour times four hours equaled 320 coils. The Kanban quantity (the quantity delivered by the vendor from the in-house store) was 500 coils. This was the number of coils agreed to by the vendor and Sally's Team. Still, other part bins in the Factory were kept filled by vendors, who would visit each day and fill the bins when levels of parts in their bins fell below the fill line. Different color bins were reserved for different vendors.

Where to Manufacture
Reorganizing Work Cells

Some parts that had been manufactured by outside vendors were brought inside to improve overall production flow. My mainframe is an example. Sally's Team determined that it was more efficient to make the mainframe in an adjacent cell rather than have a vendor manufacture the mainframes. Even though the part's cost appeared lower when purchased, it was actually *more* costly when inventory carrying costs were added back. This analysis was done for each item used in the factory. Other components that were manufactured in other parts of the factory in large batches, some far away on another floor, had their manufacturing stations moved close to their point of consumption, usually in an adjacent cell. Sometimes this required buying duplicate equipment so that the same part could be made in more than one place in the factory.

Sally says, "… let the numbers dictate where and when to manufacture an item provided you take all the variables into consideration, such as flexibility and inventory carrying cost."

Also, using a component as soon as it is made will give instant quality feedback. Rather than making power "connector sub-assemblies" the old way, which was to make a batch of 1,000 sub-assemblies in the Electronic Sub-assembly Department only to find out that something had gone wrong with an electronic component and all 1,000 sub-assemblies had to be rejected at the final inspection station at the end of the line and then reworked. The connector sub-assemblies are now made right in the Final Assembly cell. As each connector assembly is completed, it is immediately used in creating a new toaster *just* like me. This way, should there be a defect, not likely as the sub-assembly has been redesigned to reduce the number of components and eliminate errors, the defect would be detected immediately and the process could be corrected before defects were created and any rework was necessary.

Flexibility

The work cell I was created in was shaped like a U. It was designed to build 80 toasters like me an hour or 640 toasters a day; however, there was enough room so that twice as many assemblers could be added and then they could build 160 toasters an hour or 1,280 a day. Also, overtime or even a second shift could be added so that the 1,280 could be doubled again to 2,560, and if absolutely necessary a third shift could be added bringing the total capacity up to 3,840.

This eliminates the need to carry large finished goods inventories to fill orders on days when one type of toaster has a higher than usual demand. This takes the pressure off the need for an accurate forecast, which my Grandfather says "… is something that may or may not happen and usually never does."

Equipment had to be added to certain cells so that components and assemblies consumed inside the cell could be made either directly inside the cell or in a feeding cell adjacent to its consumption point. Several of my parts, like my handles, were moved to the feeder cell adjacent to my final assembly cell. This required moving a piece of molding equipment into the adjacent cell that also made my coils. Dedicating the equipment also had the effect of improving quality and saving setup costs by eliminating setups and changeovers, which took time and also left the door open to defective material resulting from errors in setting up for new runs. When more handles were required, they could be molded immediately because the material was stocked where it was used – *right* next to the molding machine and the molding machine was always setup and ready to go. Not committing raw material to the manufacturing process until shortly before it is required would contribute to flexibility by allowing that material to be used to mold other parts that may be needed.

Flexibility with labor was created by cross training all workers to do many different jobs. This was made easier by simplifying the processes so that a variety of talent could perform each task. Sally's workers loved being able to do different jobs – the variety made the work more exciting. This also made their jobs more secure. The elimination of a process would not result in layoffs. Employees could readily move into another position when needed. Employees seemed to recognize that the trade off for more job security was their willingness to learn how to perform different tasks, as well as a willingness to occasionally work flexible hours. This meant that Sally would *not* have to staff the factory for peak demand periods that would lead to frequent hiring and layoffs and would drive the cost up.

In addition to flexibility with labor and equipment, Sally needed to create flexibility with material. She did this through the agreements she made with her vendors. They agreed to keep a certain number of Kanbans on hand at all times. The Kanban level for coils was 500 coils. This was the quantity that the vendor would deliver from the in-house store when the order point of 320 was broken. The 320 represented a four hour supply – a usage of 80 an hour times the four hours it would take to deliver the coils to the consuming work cell from the in-house store. If more assemblers were added to this final assembly cell and production was to double, the vendor would receive more frequent requests for Kanban deliveries. This would not be a problem, because the coil vendor had agreed to keep enough Kanbans on hand to accommodate the increased demand. If the increased demand were to continue for an extended period, Sally's Team and the coil vendor would increase the Kanban size or the number of backup Kanbans the vendor would keep on hand. Of course, Sally's Team agreed to take responsibility for all the Kanbans held by the coil vendor in the event of a design change or a fall off in demand.

Point of use delivery was very important to Sally's plan. Vendors had to be certified based on criteria like past performance and the quality measures they took in their own facilities.   Constant monitoring of vendor quality was a key to a vendor keeping their certified status. Only a certified vendor could deliver material directly to the shop floor bypassing incoming inspection.   Sally's Team would always be looking for vendors that could deliver directly to the work cell.

By definition, all material in an in-house store had to be certified for delivery to the shop floor. The same was true for all the parts that were put directly into bins in the work cells by vendors.   Not only were the vendors required to be certified but each part had to be certified.   A vendor who supplied 20 different parts may have been certified to deliver 19 of them directly to the shop floor. The other part had to be inspected until it could be proven that the quality level was acceptable for direct shop floor delivery. Unless a vendor was certified at the vendor level, no material from that vendor would be delivered directly to the shop floor. A supplier's ability to deliver on time *consistently* was as important as their quality.

All this contributes to much lower inventories by eliminating waste, like material sitting around in kits and stockrooms for weeks on end. It puts the responsibility for material where it should be with those who can best manage it – the suppliers of the material.

Sally and her Teams' lean factory resulted in lower costs, higher quality and better delivery. Sally says, "… these are the things Customers are looking for." By the way, they are also the things Sally's Team is looking for when selecting a supplier. Sally also says, "This is the way to win new business and this is the reason Sales are up from $100,000,000 to $140,000,000 over the last few years."

Chapter 5

Chapter 5

Sally's Teams

Sally had to figure out how to execute all the new ideas she had to fix her father's factory. Adding resources was not an option because the business was already losing money. That left her with only one good option – figure out how to optimize the resources that were already available. The solution was empowering the employees already working at the factory.

Cross-Functional Self-Directed Teams were the catalyst for the empowerment process. Sally had several Teams. One addressed the elimination of "work orders" and the implementation of the new pull Kanban manufacturing system. Another Team was charged with implementing the Mistake-Proofing Program. Still another was responsible for Inventory Reduction and yet another was responsible for e-business. Later in the factory's conversion other Teams would be formed.

Sally insisted that each Team be Cross-Functional. None of the Teams had more than 12 members and some had as few as five. The Team that addressed the elimination of "work orders" and the implementation of the new Kanban pull manufacturing system had eight members. Each of the eight members was from one of these areas of the Company: Customer Service, Shipping, a Final Assembly Cell, a Feeder Cell, Purchasing, Design Engineering, Manufacturing Engineering and Accounting. Four of the members on this Team were members of four other Cross-Functional Self-Directed Teams.

This diversity of talent was required because this initiative touched virtually every area of the business. Having such diverse talent from so many areas of the business made it easy to eliminate resistance and break down barriers at the grassroots level. By including individuals who are respected by their peers, the Team's ideas were more readily accepted – the Team sold their ideas to their fellow employees. Some of the Team members would have normally been resistant to change; however; because they were part of *creating* the change, they became the project's zealots. When other employees saw that these skeptics accepted, embraced and supported the new ideas, they were easily convinced.

Each Team was empowered to draw on the other talents in the business as needed. They would sometimes request that other workers temporarily attend meetings and help on projects. One example was the time the Team had to make all the Kanban cards for the Toaster Final Assembly cell, so the Team requested the entire Accounting Department assist in making the cards. The work was done on a lunch hour and Sally bought everyone pizza – it was more like a party than work.

In addition to being "cross functional" the Teams were "Self-Directed." Self-Directed meant, just that, Self-Directed. Sally learned early that she could not rely only on herself to accomplish major initiatives. It was necessary to draw on the talents of the people that surrounded her. Sally knew that the Team concept would be far more effective without a dominating personality being present.

Optimum Team performance was fostered when all Team members participated equally in the Team process and when all Team members felt that their opinions were important. This encouraged the Team members to give their opinions freely.

Sally picked each Team Leader, Team Facilitator and then together with these individuals she picked a few candidates for Team membership. At the first Team meeting after the Team was formed, Sally addressed each Team to deliver the Team challenge. After the Team challenge had been delivered, she left the Team meeting, not to return unless invited by the Team.

Great care was taken by Sally not to interfere with the Self-Directed Teams' work. Many times this meant Sally had to bite her tongue and accept what she believed to be a mistake in the interest of noninterference.

Sally knew that once an outsider with the power to interfere and usurp the Team's authority did so, the Team would no longer be Self-Directed.

On one occasion she felt that interference was absolutely necessary, so she requested an invitation to address the Team and layout her concerns. She made the Team understand that they were the decision makers. Her guest appearance was just to make suggestions that the Team may elect to ignore. Deep down, she knew that if her guest appearance failed to gain the desired results, she would have to disband the Team and start over because at that point using her influence would neuter the Team anyway, so she would have to just start over with a fresh Team.

Sally always says, "Responsibility, accountability and authority go together; you can't have one without the other two." The policy of noninterference made the Self-Directed Teams a powerful force in the toaster business, providing all the resources necessary to drive positive and constructive change in the business.

Influencing the Team

Sally wasn't worried about having influence over the Team. She knew there were several ways for her to influence the Team's performance. The first was through the Team Leader and the Team Facilitator, both of whom she appointed when the Team was formed. One of the Team's rules was to generate minutes for each meeting. The minutes were distributed not only to the Team members, but also to Sally. In this way Sally would know what direction the Team was heading in. It was acceptable for her to attempt to influence both the Team Leader and the Team Facilitator.

The Facilitator was skilled in dealing with conflict and had the ability to deal with any conflicts in a professional manner. Sally, knowing that conflicts could arise between what the Team perceived as being in the best interest of the organization and what management perceived as being in the best interest of the organization, selected the Facilitator carefully.

Another way Sally could influence the Team was to call for a Team presentation. A very important element that contributed to the success of the "Cross-Functional Self-Directed" Team concept was the Team presentation. The Team was required to give periodic presentations to the Senior Management Team on a regular basis. The stated purpose of the presentation was to update Management on the Team's progress. The *unstated* purpose was to keep pressure on the Team to continue to make progress toward meeting the Team challenge. No one wanted to get up in front of Management during the presentation and confess that the Team had not made any progress. There was a great deal of pressure from the Teammates themselves to "get stuff done" before the presentation date so that the Team looked good to Management.

In addition to the above you could always count on human nature. There was an inclination for the Team to *want* to please Sally. She always made her position known and kept the lines of communication between senior management and the Team open, upfront and honest. The Team appreciated Management giving them free reign in meeting the challenge. They were inclined to please. And, of course, all Teams had to operate within existing company policies.

Team Training

Soon after each Team was formed the entire Team was provided with formal Team training. Sally was lucky to have a human resource leader that had experience with Team training. The training covered the various stages of Team development that most Teams go through from the kickoff stage through the productive stage. This helped the members understand what to expect in their interactions with their fellow Teammates. Other topics included:

- Why governance was important
- What was expected of the Team Leader, Team Facilitators and Team members.
- An explanation of how the Team Leader's role changes as the Team matured. The Team Leader assumed more of a Team Members role as the Team matured and leadership was not as necessary as it was when the Team was first formed.

No role was more important here than the Team Facilitator. Each Team Facilitator was given Facilitator training. Although a full member of the Team, the role of Facilitator was unique in that, the Facilitator's first responsibility was to the Team process itself.

Sally's Team Facilitators came from the Human Resource group. These folks made good facilitators because they were far enough removed from the routine day-to-day activities. They recognized that their first responsibility was to monitor the Team process. The closer an individual is to the problem at hand, the more difficult it becomes to monitor the Team process.

Sally says, "… a trained facilitator should be able to promote and encourage participation by *all* Team members, run interference with upper management, maintain fairness, help create a sense of harmony, keep the Team spirit alive, help settle internal disputes, recommend new Team members, and encourage the celebration of successes."

The Team Challenge

Sally made the Team challenges easy for everyone to understand. They were measurable, had a time limit and were important to the business' success. They were all a stretch to achieve, yet *still* achievable. Sally carefully spelled out the Team challenges for the first Teams as follows:

- Eliminate all "work orders" from the factory floor and replace them with a Kanban Pull Manufacturing system within one year.
- Implement a sustaining Mistake Proofing effort that involves all employees at all levels and delivers 5% in new realized annual savings each year.
- Reduce total inventory by 30% by the end of next year.
- Create and implement an e-business system in the next 12 months that makes it easy for customers to order direct from the factory using the internet.

All of Sally's Teams had similar characteristics. As part of each Team kickoff meeting, Sally explained the rules to all the Team members:

- Team size should be more than 5 but less than 12. With less than five people you sacrifice the benefits of having a Cross-Functional or Self-Directed Team. More than 12 Team members and the Team would become too unwieldy.

- Each Team had to be composed of a Team Leader – appointed; a Facilitator – appointed; a Secretary to keep minutes – elected; and the Team members.

- The Team had to meet at least once a week. Making this a ground rule forced the Team to meet and keep things moving.

- When a Team accomplishes its goals and the challenge was met, the Team would be disbanded. The "Cross-

Functional Self-Directed" Teams were used to define and execute major projects using the unique talents of the Team members. The work was usually over and above the Team member's every day assignments. However, the challenge was connected to the every day work the Team members were normally assigned to. *In fact*, the Team members were the beneficiaries of the successful Team outcome. Disbanding the Team when the challenge was met insured that the Team would not just go on and on leading to project creep. In this way the valuable Team recourse could be redeployed elsewhere if necessary.

- The Team was responsible for creating an infrastructure that would survive the Team effort so that the accomplishments of the Team would continue to bear fruit long after the Team has been disbanded.

- The Team sets goals and assigned tasks to meet the challenge. The Team creator, Sally, established and delivered the challenge at the first Team meeting. However, the Team set the goals that would have to be met to satisfy the challenge. It would be counter productive and presumptuous for Sally to set the Team goals for a Self-Directed Team. The nature of the on-going dynamics involved in the Teamwork dictated changing goals as the Team progressed in its work. It would not be practical to have a Self-Directed Team and have the Team creator set the goals. This would have negated the self-direction aspect of the Team.

- The Team was empowered to draw on the talents and expertise available elsewhere in the company. This included the entire organization.

- Team meeting attendance and showing up on time were both important and mandatory in order to maintain Team membership. The Team had to establish these ground rules early on, at the first or second meeting. It was a must that all Team members understand the rules. The entire Team had to agree to the boundaries. Consequences for noncompliance had to be established and adhered to from the outset. The Facilitator, usually a Human Resource professional, helped with this process.

- Teams were expected to give progress reports in the form of a presentation to a senior member of management. The presentation helped keep the project on track. This was the ultimate in Team pressure. The peer pressure to be prepared to deliver a good presentation was awesome. Nobody wanted to go before top management unprepared or with little to show for the Team's effort. This was the Team's opportunity to show off their abilities. They had a captive audience, a chance to get top management to listen. The presentations usually created an atmosphere of excitement and fun.

- Other governance ground rules were established at the outset, at the first or second meeting, by the Team.

Addressed were issues such as missing meetings without an excuse, being late for meetings regularly, consequences, majority rule, open vote verses closed vote, level of expected effort, procedure for adding members or removing members, frequency of meetings and any other issues the Team deemed necessary to cover. Sally reinforced the importance of establishing these ground rules early. She explained that although it was hoped that the mutual respect the Team members had for each other would be enough to resolve any issues that came up, it was good business practice to formalize the ground rules governing Team activities and behavior, if only to avoid any misunderstanding later.

Team Celebrations and Awards

Celebrations were a great way to say thanks and encourage more of the same results that would bring more celebrations. Sally encouraged Teams to celebrate even the small successes. They were kept simple – a cake and coffee break or a pizza party. An acknowledgement for a job well done was the important thing – just saying THANKS.

In addition to the minor celebrations along the Team's path to meeting the challenge, Sally gave each Team member a $1,000 cash award. What a hit that was! The Team members talked about that gesture for months.

Sometimes the Team had the company cafeteria prepare dinners to be taken home for the spouses of the Team members that had to work late on a project. This only cost the company a few dollars for each dinner and demonstrated to the Team member's families that the company recognized and was appreciative of the sacrifice the whole family was making in order to help create a stronger more secure employment situation for all involved. Employees said "It made them look like heroes in their family's eyes."

One of the nicest benefits of forming Cross-Functional Self-Directed Teams was their ability to breakdown traditional barriers between departments. Team members were placed in situations where they had to rely and depend on each other's talents and skills to succeed as a Team. There was nothing like these types of situations to harvest respect for fellow employees. Just becoming familiar with a co-worker's responsibilities and daily challenges brought an understanding between individuals and groups. Development of mutual respect is a natural byproduct of an entire Team drawn from different areas of the business, pulling in the same direction to achieve a common goal.

The "Cross-Functional Self-Directed" Teams fostered camaraderie and the goodwill created far outlasted the Teams or their efforts. The friendships and relationships developed through the Teamwork spilled over into the other day-to-day activities in the rest of the business. Some of the relationships between employees even spilled over into their personal lives. Some joined professional organizations together and others went to school together nights.

Employees developed a sense of ownership when asked to resolve a major issue that deeply affected the company's success. The project became their baby. They wanted to see that nothing adverse happened that would negatively affect their baby. And, of course, when a Team member got close to a project, they got closer to the entire company. The more they had invested in the company, the more interested they were about the overall health of the company.

The Toaster factory ended up with better, longer-lasting improvements that were implemented much quicker. With limited resources, where did the company get the talent they needed to run the day-to-day business while at the same time making great improvements on a grand scale? The answer was Sally's "Cross-Functional Self-Directed" Teams.

EPILOGUE: A FINAL WORD

Don't just put this book down and go back to doing business as usual.

- *Take a look at your business*
- *Compare your own business processes to the ones described in this book*
- *Get your employees involved in converting your business into a lean money-making enterprise.*

Actions say more than words and your words must be backed by actions. Your Company can achieve similar results or even greater results. Your employees can do it for you. Just ask them, they are ready to help.

Glossary of Terms

<u>Backflushing</u> – A process that utilizes the bill-of-material to determine the material used to manufacture an item in the product structure, and then subtracts that material from inventory thus eliminating the keying of each part used to manufacture the item.

<u>Brainstorming</u> – A powerful technique used by small groups to generate spontaneous ideas in order to solve a problem. The group records, then discusses whatever problem solving ideas pop into their head. As a rule no idea is a bad idea and the group should consider each idea.

Cause and effect diagram (fish bone diagram) – A problem solving tool in the form of a diagram that illustrates the relationship between the outcome and the factors that affect it. The outcome is placed at the head of the centerline on the diagram and the elements that influence the outcome are placed on lines connected to the centerline. The elements are usually grouped in categories such as Materials, Methods, Machines, Measurements, Personnel and Environment, each Category having its own line connecting to the centerline.

DMAIC method – A structured process of applying Six Sigma methodology to improve processes. DMAIC includes the following steps: Defining the problem/opportunity, Measuring the results, Analyzing the measurements to determine what needs to be corrected to improve the process, Improving the process by making the necessary changes and Controlling the circumstances so that the process remains fixed.

Failure Mode and Effects Analysis (FMEA) – A proactive technique used to help anticipate and reduce failures. The process helps determine what problems could occur, the consequences of those problems, the frequency at which the problem is likely to occur, the severity of the problem occurring and the likelihood of detecting the problem. Values are assigned to the frequency, severity and detectability of each occurrence (usually on a scale from 1 to 10) to help determine which items need immediate attention and or mitigation.

First-Pass Yield – The number of units that make it through your final test station without incident (usually expressed as a %).

Poka-yoke – Mistake Proofing – A Japanese term meaning "fool proofing," which uses product and process design to create conditions that greatly reduce the possibility of a process error by either giving immediate feedback that an error is about to occur or an error has just occurred or preventing the possibility of an error occurring altogether.

<u>Self-Directed Cross-Functional Team</u> – Team composed of members from different functions in the business in order to meet a challenge assigned to them. This Team meets regularly and frequently reports the Team's progress to top management through minutes and periodic presentations. The Team has considerable freedom and operates independent of the company's functional management.

<u>Six Sigma</u> – A methodology that facilitates determining the actions necessary in optimizing and correcting business processes by eliminating variation, thereby increasing profits, and eliminating defects and waste.

<u>Statistical Process Control</u> – A method of monitoring a process to detect and predict the probability of defects occurring in that process.

Sources

Buckley, Ronald L., Winning in a Highly Competitive Manufacturing Environment, Shady Brook Press, 2003

Buckley, Ronald L. and Buckley, Candace Lynn, No Eraser Needed – Mistake Proofing Your Business, 2007 Sax Macy Fromm

Galsworth, Gwendolyn D., The Visual Systems: Harnessing the Power of a Visual Workplace, AMACOM, American Management Association, 1997.

Greif, Michel, The Visual Factory: Building Participation Through Shared Information, Productivity Press, Inc., Portland, Oregon, 1991.

Katzenbach, Jon R. and Smith, Douglas K., The Wisdom of Teams: Creating the High-Performance Organization, Harper Business – Division of Harper Collins Publishers, New York, New York, 1994.

Pande, Peter S., Neuman, Robert P. and Cavanagh, Roland R., The Six Sigma Way, McGraw-Hill Company, New York, New York, 2000.

Schonberger, Richard J., World Class Manufacturing: The Next Decade, Building Power, Strength, and Value, The Free Press, 1996.

Shigeo Shingo, Zero Quality Control: Source Inspection and the Poka-yoke System, Productivity Press, Stamford, CT and Cambridge, MA, 1986.

Appendices

I have included several appendices here that can be easily adapted to fit your own business improvement strategy. They pretty much follow the material presented in the book. Copy them, change them and turn them into your own presentations if you like. They are:

•Appendix A – Manufacturing. The factory

•Appendix B – Quality

•Appendix C – Self-Directed Teams

•Appendix D – Cost Savings Check List

Appendix A

Manufacturing

Appendix A

Manufacturing
The Factory
R L Buckley

The Lean Path to
Continuous Improvement

The Way I See It

- Never let any subcontractor get close to your Customers
- Get your Low Cost Country (LCC) suppliers to use a local freight forwarder to hold inventory you can draw on -- Kanban
- Upper-level assembly, test, configuration in your own factory LCC or High Cost Country (HCC) – be the best here!!
- Distribution to customers from your own facilities –
- Be "World Class"
  - Highest quality - 99%+ first-pass yield – eliminate Out-of-Box Failures
  - Lowest possible cost - flow manufacturing
  - On-time delivery - within 5 day - first goal
  - Velocity (product throughput to 3 days)
  - Real self-directed work teams

Flow Manufacturing

Lean Flow Kanban pull system - no work orders

- Customer ⇐ finished goods ⇐ factory Kanban ⇐ vendor Kanban
- Linked cell manufacturing
- Inventory flexibility/reduction
- "In-house store", "Bread Man routine", "Wand to order"
- Point of use material delivery
- Certified vendors
- No WIP material -- cycle counting -- backflushing
- Manufacturing elements: labor, material, equipment
- Training – flexibility

---

3 Ways To Build

Moving product and material through factory

1. Work order – push
   - Schedule in the future based on forecast
   - Kit material
   - Charge labor
   - Sometimes assign to equipment
2. Dispatching – push
   - Schedule in the future based on forecast
   - Pull material when ready to build
   - May or may not charge labor and assign equipment
3. Lean flow - Pull - Kanban signal – maximum flexibility
   - Build only when there is a demand
   - Pull material only when needed
   - Many other ways to charge labor

Pull System

- Customer places demand on finished goods
  - Finished goods demand fill causes signal
  - Signal causes factory demand
  - Factory demand fill causes signal
  - Signal causes vendor demand
  - Vendor demand fill causes signal
    - In-house store
    - Bread Man routine
    - Wand to order
  - Vendor signal fill creates PO – fills PO – creates Accounts Payable

Linked Cell Manufacturing

- Form each cell
  - U-shaped cells
  - Benches form the U
  - From left to right or right to left – be consistent
  - Define assembly flow – flow chart
  - Product size, number of parts, volume and demand variability will dictate cell size – 500 square feet is nice
  - Number of units per day
  - Design cell for flexibility
  - Link the cell by proximity to all the cells that supply this cell and also to the cell this cell supplies

Linked cell Kanbans

Linked cell signals

- Use one week – simple
- Use formula only when absolutely necessary
- Two-bin system is easiest
  - Bin travels as signal to make more
  - One weeks inventory between the bins
  - Use multiple bins to set priorities – FG Kanbans
    1. 5 of 5 bins part X back home – stock out!
    2. 4 of 5 bins part Y back home – make part 1 first
- Card Signal
  - Order point – 5 left then send card to make 10
  - Scan card sends message - intranet - internet – fax server

---

Inventory Flexibility/Reduction

- Create flexibility
  - Always have what I need when I need it!
  - I don't care when you make it – just have it when I need it!
- Make inventory your vendor's problem:
  - In-house stores
    - Consignment
  - Bread Man routine
  - Wand to order
- Increasing velocity pulls material through faster
- Make your LCC suppliers use freight forwarders to hold THEIR inventory

Use these techniques and watch your inventory disappear

RL BUCKLEY   Velocity

- Measured in days
- Starts when the first component is placed
- Ends when the unit is stocked
- Data must be collected automatically – Wanding
- When the unit is transacted to stock can look at history of longest lead assembly – is the birthing date
- The above requires a bar code assignment to the item when the assembly starts – this is then the birthing date

---

RL BUCKLEY   In-house Store

- You provide designated floor space for material
- Vendor provides material
- Vendor provides Stock Keeper
- Also works for consignment material without Stock Keeper
- Vendor manages their inventory
- Scan into your inventory when delivered to your floor
- Vendor responsible for supplying inventory when you need it
- Vendor signal fill creates PO – fills PO – creates Accounts Payable
- Works well with electronic components, etc.
- Letter of intent with a partnering vendor

Bread Man Routine

- Used primarily for low value items
- Make your vendor responsible for filling all the blue bins or red bins or green bins, etc.
- Vendors visit daily - fill the bins that have reached fill level
- Vendor responsible for supplying inventory when you need it
- Vendor signal fill creates PO – fills PO – creates Accounts Payable
- Works well for nuts, bolts and screws, raw cable, resistors, etc.
- Letter of intent with a partnering vendor

Wand To Order

- Shop Floor operator uses bar code scanner to scan a Kanban bar code when a level is reached
- Message sent to PC or fax server
- Message sent to vendor
- Vendor delivers next day to Shop Floor (if certified part and certified vendor)
- Parts received with scanner Vendor responsible for supplying material when you need it
- Vendor signal fill creates PO – fills PO – creates Accounts Payable
- Works well with sheet-metal, packaging materials, circuit boards, cable assemblies, manuals, etc.
- Letter of intent with a partnering vendor

109

Letter Of Intent

- Letter of intent with a partnering vendor
  - Annual usage by part (within range) - access to your changing requirements
  - Pricing agreement
  - When pay – (50 to 60 days after taking possession)
  - Vendor must supply at the same or better price than you can buy anywhere – you must be reasonable
  - Can bundle commodities
  - Re-quote every year – ongoing
  - Provides for discontinuation responsibility

Point Of Use

- Deliver material to the work cell whenever possible
- Store inventory in the cell at the point of use
- Same parts used in more than one cell - highest usage gets the delivery – Production Associates access from other cells
- Keep Kanbans small enough
- Do not over stock
- May need warehouse for bulky items
- Warehouse linked to cell
- Never sacrifice efficiency in cell for storage
- Should be able to see all 4 walls

Certified Vendors

- Only certified vendors can deliver directly to the cell
- Certification program in line with your other quality programs
  - Historical quality record
  - ISO qualifications
  - On-site inspections
  - Questionnaire compliance
- After certifying vendor - must certify each part supplied
  - part's quality history and manufacturing location history
- Material not certified must be inspected according to current IQA criteria

No WIP Material

- Your factory becomes your stockroom
- All material is considered either:
  - Raw material
  - Finished goods
- Parts are scanned onto Shop Floor (stockroom) from:
  - In-house store
  - Bread Man – can be expensed
  - Wand to order delivery
- The backflushing process removes the material when finished goods is scanned to stock
- The material stocked in the cells is cycle counted daily to the cycle count plan – by cell Production Associates

Monitoring Labor Costs

Labor Absorption

- Use standard cost
- Know what you built
- Collect labor from time and attendance records
- Compare – unit standard X quantity built to hours worked
- Standard X quantity greater than hours worked = over absorbed
- Standard X quantity less that hours worked = under absorbed

---

Creating Flexibility

- Labor – material – equipment
- Equipment flexibility – given – not working 3 shifts 7 days a week – have equipment flexibility with OT
- Material flexibility – previously created material flexibility
- Labor flexibility – must be created with training

Labor Flexibility = Training

Today I built Mills. Yesterday I built boards. Tomorrow I
will be winding film in the morning and testing fetal
monitors in the afternoon. ===== THIS IS REAL!

- Reward for skills learned
- List employees and their skills – visible, well
maintained
- Offer training on your time all the time
  - Plan it - schedule it - make training mandatory
    and optional
  - Training on entry
    - Flow manufacturing
    - Component Identification
    - As well as technical skills i.e. Soldering skills

Andon Lights

- 4" high by 30" long dot matrix displays products
- The product names either green, yellow, or red - depending on
the production/shipping status
  - Yellow will indicate a pending problem
  - Green means go, no problems
  - Red will indicate unable to ship, all hands on deck
- Displayed in:
  - Purchasing   Q/A R/A
  - Cafeteria   Manufacturing
  - Order Management   Engineering
  - Management Offices Manufacturing Engineering
- Controlled by Shop Floor Supervisor

Lean Manufacturing

- **QA organization**
  - Eliminate QA inspectors
  - Don't build in lots, sort out rejects, use good ones
  - Statistical Process Control (SPC) put operator in charge of quality
  - Poka-yoke -- train all the people
- **Data collection -- bar code**
  - DHR, critical components
  - Backflushing
  - Kanban signals to vendor
  - Quality related tracking and identification (OBF, teams)
- **Warranty expense less than 1% of revenue**

Lean Manufacturing

To be "World Class"
Cannot rest on past accomplishments

- Inventory turns must be increased to 25
- On-time delivery increased to 100% level
- First-pass yield increased to 99%+
- Throughput time decreased to 3 to 4 days
- Warranty/scrap expense kept under 1%

Appendix B

Quality

Appendix B

Quality

Path to Continuous Improvement

R L Buckley

RL BUCKLEY First-Pass Yield

Recommend a Team approach
- Measure after burn
- Plug the unit in and it works
- No tweaking
- Unit is ready to be configured
- 99% yield here reflects cumulative yield of all assemblies
- Keep it simple and Production Associates will manage it
- More than three failures in a cell in a day alerts Team members of a problem – should be automatic and electronic – to their desktop or pager/cell phone

Get this over 99% and Watch your OBFs disappear

First-Pass Yield

Quality related tracking and identification:
- – Track each component that fails at final test
- – Summarize and categorize all data
- – Analyze and look for commonality
- – Add Sub Assembly Groups to the Team
- – Add vendors of problem parts to the Team
- – Recommend Engineering changes
- – Don't build assemblies in lots, sort out rejects, use good ones – build all assemblies in the final assembly cell
- – SPC - put operator in charge of quality, if they are not already

Your Production Associates Will Be Key To Success

First-Pass Yield

Eliminate Workmanship Errors
- • Poka-yoke the process -- train all the people
  - – Make it formal
  - – The course is inexpensive
  - – You could teach it in house
    - » Two day course
    - » You can buy the course material
    - . Simple and easy to understand examples
      - . Your Production Associates will love it

Workmanship Errors Are The Easiest To Fix

117

Customer Quality Metrics

Customer's wants – the basics:
- Acceptable quality - on-time delivery - low cost
  - You control quality
  - You control delivery
  - You control cost
- You are concerned with all but try to measure what you control.
- DOA / OBF – Breakdown by:
  - » Design failures
  - » Random component failures
  - » No problem found
  - » Workmanship
  - Insist DOA / OBFs are returned
  - Insist on your Team reviewing DOA / OBF returns

Customer Quality Metrics

- Warranty expense:
  - Service breakdown by product
  - Difficult numbers to get – be persistent
  - Drive to less than 1%
- Install
  - Who gets this feedback?
  - What kind of feedback is available?
  - Website or questionnaire?
  - Select the data
  - This can be part of your closed loop feedback

Two Issues: Customer Satisfaction and Profits

Customer Quality/Satisfaction

- Delivery:
  - SPAN – this is the chosen metric for delivery
  - Ship Complete On Time (SCOT) to the Customer promise – do it!
    - Distinguishes your operation from the rest
    - Allows focus on the problem areas
      - Unreasonable promises
      - Unreleased product being sold
      - Product delayed from Low Cost Country (LCC)
      - Always ship complete
      - Need personal permission of Plant Manager to ship incomplete order - – - measure this
    - A short ship is an OBF – easy to fix

Six Sigma

Six Sigma Utilization

On The

Lean Path To Continuous Improvement

Defining 6 Sigma

What is Six Sigma?

- Measuring and eliminating the variations in any process.
- Sigma = standard deviation
  - 2 sigma   308,537   DPMO
  - 3 sigma   66,807   DPMO
  - 4 sigma   6210   DPMO
  - 5 sigma   233   DPMO
  - 6 sigma   3.4 DPMO

Improve your process 3 sigma to 6 sigma - 20,000 times improvement!

Which airplane do you want to fly on?

---

6 Sigma Methodology?

Why do we care about 6 Sigma methodology?

- If you can't measure or you don't measure, you will never know and understand your process
- If you don't know and understand your processes, you will never control or improve your processes
- You will forever be relying on chance and dumb luck

Serving Your Customers

Deliver:

Higher quality products

At a lower cost

On-time – when your Customer wants them

Be The Best – Leap Frog Your Competition

RL BUCKLEY Areas Of 6 Sigma Application

- Manufacturing
- Engineering – product design
- Back office
  - Order Management
  - Finance
  - Collections and Payables
  - e-business
  - RA/QA
- Marketing & Sales
- Service

Apply To All Business Functions – Identify Deviations From The Ideal

What Is In It For Your People?

Not just fun – and it is fun!!

- An investment in your employees
- Personal growth
- Everybody wants to be the best and work for the best
- Attract the best
- A skill that is in high demand
- Eliminate the politics in project decisions

Some Of The 6 Sigma Tools

Examples of tools used:

- ✓ Benchmarking
- ✓ Brainstorming
- ✓ Control charts
- ✓ Capability analysis
- ✓ Histogram – frequency distribution
- ✓ Pareto – sort vital few from trivial many
- ✓ QFD Quality function deployment – VOC in design
- ✓ FMEA – failure mode and effects analysis
- ✓ Gage R&R – Gage repeatability and reproductibility
- ✓ Process Mapping
- ✓ DOE – Design of experiments
- ✓ C & E – Cause and Effect

"The problems that exist in the world of today...

...Cannot be solved by the level of thinking that created them."
   Albert Einstein

Appendix C

Self-Directed Teams

Self-Directed Teams

Path to Continuous Improvement

R L Buckley

RL BUCKLEY   **Self-Directed Teams**

- Establish a challenge -- Should be established by the person forming the Team. The following are examples for self-directed (cross-functional) Teams:
  - 1. Reduce inventory by $10,000,000 by the end of the year
  - 2. Improve on-time delivery hit rate to the 99%+ level over the next year
  - 3. Eliminate the use of Shop Floor work orders by December
  - 4. Automate the Data Collection systems on the Manufacturing Floor - up and running by January 1
- Each Team is composed of: a Team Leader - appointed; a Facilitator - appointed; a Secretary to keep minutes - elected; and the Team members
- Team size usually should be more than 5 less than 12

RL BUCKLEY   Self-Directed Teams

- Teams should meet at least once a week
- When Teams accomplish their goals, the Team will be disbanded
- Team must create an infrastructure that will survive the Team effort so that the accomplishments of the Team will continue to bear fruit
- Team sets goals and assigns tasks to meet the challenge
- Each Team is empowered to draw on the talents and expertise in the Company (this includes the entire organization) on a part-time basis. For example: If help is required from the Sourcing Group to get vendor quotes, a buyer will be assigned to the Team until the quoting is complete

---

RL BUCKLEY   Self-Directed Teams

- Team meeting attendance and showing up on time is both important and mandatory in order to maintain Team member status

- Teams are expected to give progress reports to a senior manager (the more senior the better) in the form of a Team presentation

- Governance ground rules should be established up front – at the first or second meeting - by the Team, as the Team deems necessary. The ground rules could cover majority rule, attendance, etc.

Appendix D

Cost Savings

Cost Savings Check List

Path to Continuous Improvement
R L Buckley

- Labor hours
  - Overtime reduction
  - Temps, contractors
  - Process improvement
  - Shift elimination
- Outsource – vendor does it at a lower cost
- Review all equipment leases
  - Copiers
  - Shipping dock
  - Trucks & cars
  - Storage trailers

Cost Savings Check List 2

- Services
  - Carpets
  - Equipment servicing
    - Fork trucks
    - Bailers
- Off-site storage
  - Building leases
- Scrap
- Quote boards and/or assemblies outside
- Shop supplies
  - ESD Shop Coats
  - Small tools – add to in-house stores

Cost Savings Check List 3

- Depreciation
  - Unneeded assets that can be transferred or sold
  - Non-existent assets
- Freight
  - Look for vendors with several freight charges on the same day. Charging freight for two deliveries when both items came in the same box.
  - When we pay the freight – only when we agreed
  - When ship – ship lowest cost – etc.
- Calibration
  - Outside vs. inside
  - Remove unused items from service
- Utilities
  - Phones – cell phones
  - Electric
  - Water
  - Gas

RL BUCKLEY Cost Savings Check List 4

- Housekeeping
- Obsolescence
- Product packaging
- Travel & Entertainment
- Discretionary meetings
- Supplies
- Shop Floor space you pay for and maybe don't use
- Cafeteria contributions – is it allocated?
- Other allocated expenses you do not control
- Purchase costs
  - CDs - inside or outside
  - Manuals - inside or outside